ACHIEVE LEVEL 5

MATHEMATICS

Louise Moore

Series editor: **Richard Cooper**

Rising Stars UK Ltd, 7 Hatchers Mews, Bermondsey Street, London SE1 3GS

www.risingstars-uk.com

All facts are correct at time of going to press.

First published 2002
Second edition 2008
This edition 2010
Reprinted 2011 (twice)

First edition written by: Richard Cooper
Illustrations: Tim Oliver and Clive Wakfer
Design: Clive Sutherland
Cover design: Burville-Riley Partnership

British Library Cataloguing in Publication Data
A CIP record for this book is available from the British Library.

ISBN 978-1-84680-776-3

Printed by Craft Print International Ltd, Singapore

Contents

How to use this book

What we have included:

★ Those topics at Level 4 that are trickiest to get right ('the tricky bits').

★ ALL Level 5 content so you know that you are covering all the topics that you need to understand in order to achieve Level 5.

★ A selection of our favourite test techniques, tips for revision and some advice on what the National Tests are all about, as well as the answers so you can see how you are getting on.

(1) Introduction – This section tells you what you need to do to get a Level 5. It picks out the key learning objective and explains it simply.

(2) Self-assessment – Tick the face that best describes your understanding of this concept.

(3) Question – The question helps you to learn by doing. It is presented in a similar way to a National Test question and gives you a real example to work with.

(4) Flow chart – This shows you the steps to use when completing questions like this. Some of the advice appears on every flow chart (e.g. 'Read the question then read it again'). This is because this is the best way of getting good marks in the test.

(5) Tip boxes – These provide test hints and general tips on getting the best marks in the National Tests.

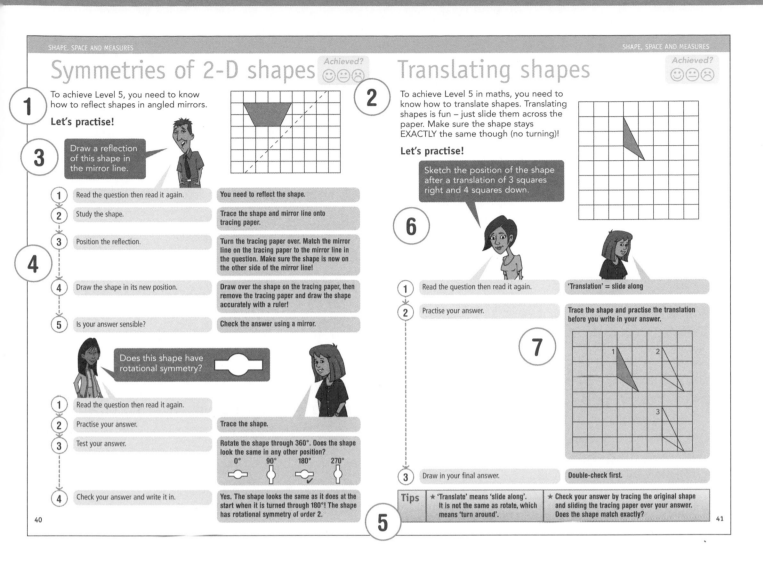

(6) **Second question** – On some pages there will be a second question. This will either look at a slightly different question type or give you another example to work through.

(7) **Practice questions** – This is where you have to do the work! Try each question using the technique in the flow chart then check your answers at the back of the book. Practising questions is the best way to help improve your understanding.

GOOD LUCK!

Key facts

NUMBER AND ALGEBRA
Counting and understanding number

Place value
- Each number is made up of digits. The position of the digit in a number gives its value.

Hundreds	Tens	Units	tenths	hundredths
7	8	4	3	5

$$= 700 + 80 + 4 + \tfrac{3}{10} + \tfrac{5}{100} = 784.35$$

Estimating
- When rounding, remember that 5 goes up! 6.785 rounds up to 6.79.

Positive and negative integers
- Integers are just whole numbers.
- When counting from negative up to positive or from positive down to negative, **remember to count 0!**
- When counting on a number line, count to the right when adding and to the left when subtracting.

Fractions
- The numerator tells you how many equal parts are used.
- The denominator tells you how many equal parts there are.
- A fraction is used to express a proportion or part.

Reducing a fraction to its simplest form
- To reduce a fraction to its simplest form (or lowest terms), find a common factor which you can divide into the numerator and the denominator. For example,

$$\frac{3 \div 3}{9 \div 3} = \frac{1}{3}$$

Fraction, decimal and percentage equivalents
- Remember as many of these as you can.

Fraction	$\frac{1}{2}$	$\frac{1}{10}$	$\frac{1}{4}$	$\frac{3}{4}$	Nearly $\frac{1}{3}$
Decimal	0.5	0.1	0.25	0.75	0.33
Percentage	50%	10%	25%	75%	33%

The vocabulary of ratio and proportion
- Ratio is 'to every'.
- Proportion is 'in every'.
- Reduce ratios and proportions to their simplest form.

Knowing and using number facts
- **Tables:** it is essential that you know these really well.
- **Squares:** numbers made when a number is multiplied by itself.
- **Multiples:** numbers that have been multiplied by a given number.
- **Factors:** numbers that can divide into a given number without leaving a remainder.

Checking your answers
- Inverse means opposite!
- Check addition by subtraction – and vice versa.
- Check division by multiplication – and vice versa.
- Use 'friendly numbers' when estimating: 2, 5, 10, etc.

Calculating
- Multiplying numbers by 10 and 100: push the digits to the left once for ×10 and twice for ×100.
- Dividing numbers by 10 and 100: push the digits to the right once for ÷10 and twice for ÷100.
- Addition and subtraction of decimals:
  1. Line up the decimal points when you write out the calculation.
  2. Fill empty places with a 0.
  3. Remember to put the decimal point in your answer!
- Multiplication and division of decimals:
  1. × and ÷ are opposites
  2. There must be the same number of digits after the decimal point in the answer as there are altogether in the question.

Brackets
- Always do the brackets in equations first.

Choosing your method
- Remember to look at the numbers you are working with. You might be able to use a good mental strategy rather than a written method, or it might be best to use a calculator.

SHAPE, SPACE AND MEASURES
Understanding shape

3-D shapes
- Vertices are corners.
- Faces are flat surfaces.
- Edges are edges!

2-D shapes

- Polygons have all straight sides.
- Regular polygons have sides all the same length.
- Parallel lines never meet – think of a train track!
- Perpendicular lines make a right angle.

Triangles

- An isosceles triangle has TWO EQUAL SIDES AND TWO EQUAL ANGLES. Picture an isosceles triangle as an arrow!
- A scalene triangle has THREE SIDES OF DIFFERENT LENGTHS and THREE ANGLES OF DIFFERENT SIZES. When picturing a scalene triangle, think of scaling a mountain that has an easy way up or a more difficult side to climb!
- A right-angled triangle can be isosceles or scalene.

Moving 2-D shapes

- When drawing reflections, remember to keep the correct distance from the mirror line.
- Remember, rotational symmetry is just working out how many ways the shape can fit EXACTLY on top of itself.
- When translating a shape move it across first, then up or down.

Angles

- Acute angle is between 0° and 89°
- Right angle = 90°
- Obtuse angle is between 91° and 179°
- Straight line = 180°
- Reflex angle is between 181° and 359°

Coordinates

- Always read ALONG the x axis and then UP/DOWN the y axis.
- Always write (x) before (y), i.e. (x, y).

Measuring

Metric and imperial conversions (approx.)

- 1 litre = 1.8 pints
- 1 kilogram = 2.2 lbs (pounds)
- 1 pound = 0.454 kg
- 1 mile = 1.6 km
- 5 miles = 8 km

- 1 foot = 30 cm
- 1 metre = 3 feet 3 inches
- 1 inch = 2.5 cm

Measures

- Milli = $\frac{1}{1000}$
- Centi = $\frac{1}{100}$
- Cent = 100
- Kilo = 1000

Perimeter

- Perimeter is the distance all the way round the edge of a flat shape.

Area

- Area is the space covered up by the shape.
- Count the squares. Remember area is always measured in square units (cm², mm², m²).

Area of a rectangle

- Area of a rectangle = length (L) × width (W)

Reading scales

- CAREFULLY work out what each mark on the scale is worth.

HANDLING DATA

Pictograms

- With pictograms PICTURE = NUMBER

e.g. ▽ = 20 ice creams ⌇ = 10 ice creams

Mean, median, range, mode

- Mean = sum of all values divided by number of values
- Median = middle number in sequence (always write down in order first)
- Range = difference between highest and lowest number
- Mode = most common value

Charts and graphs

- Be careful and accurate. Use a sharp pencil.
- Pie charts are good for percentages, fractions or decimals.

Probability scale

- Always goes from 0 to 1 (so you need fractions/decimals).

impossible	less likely	even chance	more likely	certain
0	0.25	0.5	0.75	1

USING AND APPLYING MATHEMATICS

Simple formulae

- Talk through the formula in your head. It will make it easier.

Number patterns

- Check the difference between the numbers to find the pattern.

About the National Tests

Key facts

★ The Key Stage 2 National Tests take place in the summer term in Year 6. You will be tested on Maths and English.

★ The tests take place in your school and will be marked by examiners – not your teacher!

★ Individual test scores are not made public but a school's combined scores are published in what are commonly known as 'league tables'.

The Maths National Tests

You will take three tests in Maths:

● **Mental Maths Test** – This test will be played to you on an audio CD. You will have to answer the questions mentally within 5, 10 or 15 seconds. This test will take about 20 minutes.

● **Test A** – The non-calculator test. This test requires quick answers on a test paper. You will not be able to use a calculator but should show any working you do.

● **Test B** – This test allows you to use a calculator and includes problems that will take you longer to solve. If you do calculations on the calculator, remember to write down what you did. You might get a mark for the correct method, even if you get the answer wrong. Remember, the calculator is only as a good as the person who uses it!

DON'T FORGET!

Using and applying mathematics
There are many questions testing how you use and apply your mathematical knowledge in different situations. This includes:
• knowing which is the important information in the questions
• how to check your results
• describing things mathematically using common symbols and diagrams
• explaining your reasons for conclusions that you make.

Much of the book is written to help you practise for these questions. See also pages 53–60, which should help you with this area of maths.

You might be asked to explain your answers and also write possible answers. Remember, always show your method.

Predicting sequences

To achieve Level 4, you need to know how to predict sequences. This is not as difficult as it sounds. Sequences and patterns just can't live without each other!

Just remember: sequence = numbers following a pattern.

Pattern 1 The pattern may mean the difference between numbers is always the same:

2	4	6	8	10

+2 +2 +2 +2

Pattern 2 The pattern may mean that the difference between numbers changes according to a rule:

5	11	23	41	65

+6 +12 +18 +24

Let's practise!

Predict the next two numbers in this sequence:

5, 18, 31, 44, ☐ , ☐

1 Read the question then read it again.

What is the pattern?

2 Study the numbers.

What is the difference between the numbers?
5 + ? = 18   ? = 13
18 + ? = 31   ? = 13

3 Test the pattern.

Is the difference always 13?
  5   18   31   44   57   70
   +13 +13 +13 +13 +13

4 Does the pattern work? If so, write in the next two numbers.

Yes, the pattern works and the next numbers in the sequence are 57 and 70.

Practice questions
Find the missing numbers in these sequences:

1 23, 35, 47, ☐ , ☐

2 2, ☐ , 12, ☐ , 22

3 9, 5, ☐ , ☐ , –7

4 5, ☐ , ☐ , 23

Tips	★ You will see the pattern more easily if you write each difference underneath the sequence.	★ A sequence may be shown in pictures. Just turn the pictures into numbers to help you see the pattern.

4   14   34   64
 +10 +20 +30

★   ★★   ★★   ★★★★
               ★★   ★★★
1   2   4   7
   +1   +2   +3

Perimeter

To achieve Level 4, you need to be able to calculate perimeters. A common mistake is to miss one of the sides of the shape.

> The perimeter is the total distance around the outside of a shape.

Let's practise!

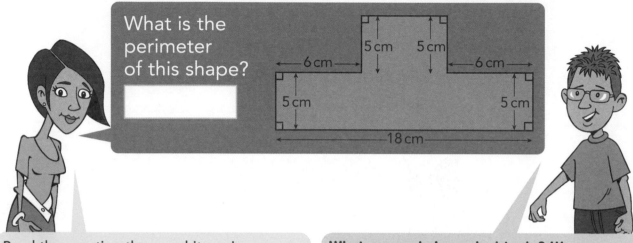

What is the perimeter of this shape?

	1	Read the question then read it again.	What are we being asked to do? We are being asked to measure the distance around the shape.
	2	Choose a side to start from. Put a line through it with your pencil.	This helps you to remember where you started from.
	3	Add up all the lengths that are given in the question. Mark them off as you go.	5 cm + 6 cm + 5 cm + 18 cm + 5 cm + 6 cm + 5 cm = 50 cm
	4	Now work out the lengths of the sides you haven't been given.	This is the IMPORTANT PART! The right angles show you that the distance along the top of the shape must be the same as the distance along the bottom. Both must be 18 cm. The missing side must be 6 cm because 6 cm + 6 cm + 6 cm = 18 cm.
	5	Add the unknown length to the total of the lengths you have been given (see step 3).	50 cm + 6 cm = 56 cm
	6	Is your answer a sensible one? If so, put it in the box.	The perimeter of the shape is 56 cm.

Tips	★ Think of a perimeter fence going all the way round a football pitch.	★ Don't try to measure the missing sides with a ruler. The diagrams are not drawn to scale, so you will not get the correct answer!

The 24-hour clock

Achieved?

To achieve Level 4, you need to be a time expert. You should be pretty good at telling the time by now, but certain questions can still cause problems. It's very easy to make silly mistakes when working with the 24-hour clock.

Let's practise!

How long is it from 03:14 to 21:26?

1	Read the question then read it again.	
2	Picture the question.	Imagine the times. 03:14 is very early in the morning; 21:26 is late evening. The answer will be quite large.
3	Count the minutes round to the first hour.	03:14 to 04:00 is 46 minutes.
4	Now count the hours round to the given hour.	04:00 around to 21:00 is 17 hours.
5	Add up the minutes and convert to hours if you need to.	46 minutes + the 26 minutes (from the time 21:26) is 72 minutes. 72 minutes = 1 hour and 12 minutes.
6	Calculate all the hours and add the remaining minutes to give a final answer.	17 hours + 1 hour + 12 minutes = 18 hours and 12 minutes.
7	Does the answer look sensible? If so, put it in the box.	Yes, our answer looks sensible. 18 hours and 12 minutes is correct.

Practice questions

1 How long is it from 09:46 to 14:31?

2 How long is it from 15:48 to 23:15?

3 It takes Hannah 5 hours and 22 minutes to travel from home to London.

If she sets off at 21:45, what time will she arrive?

Tips	★ Get used to reading timetables for buses, trains and aeroplanes. Test yourself on imaginary journeys.	★ Remember, when comparing times the fastest one is the shortest one.

Reading scales

Achieved?

To achieve Level 4, you have to use scales to measure things. They are just like number lines! The trick is to remember to work out what each mark stands for.

Let's practise!

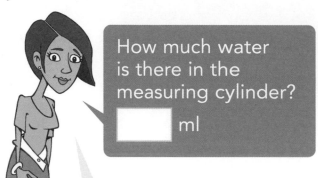

How much water is there in the measuring cylinder?

☐ ml

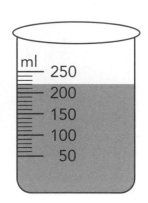

ml
— 250
— 200
— 150
— 100
— 50

1 Read the question then read it again.

2 Picture the numbers.

The answer is between 200 ml and 250 ml.

3 Study the scale.

Count the gaps made by the small lines between 200 ml and 250 ml. There are 5 gaps. We therefore know that 5 gaps must equal 50 ml.

4 Calculate the scale.

5 gaps = 50 ml
1 gap = 10 ml (50 ÷ 5)

5 Answer the question.

Water level is at 200 ml plus 2 gaps
= 200 ml + 20 ml
= 220 ml

6 If your answer looks sensible, write it in the box.

If not, go back to step 2 and try again.

Practice questions

Which numbers are the arrows pointing to on this scale?

A ☐   B ☐   C ☐

0   A ↓ 1km   B ↓   2 km   C ↓   3 km

| Tips | ★ Read scales very carefully and count the gaps more than once to be sure you have got it right. Write in missing measurements in pencil to help you remember them. | ★ Always check your answer carefully to be sure it makes sense. |

Venn diagrams

To achieve Level 4, you need to be able to read all kinds of sorting diagrams.

Venn diagrams may sound complicated but really they are just a way of sorting information into groups. Look at the diagram. There are three regions – **A**, **B** and **C**.

Region **A** belongs to group A.

Region **B** belongs to group B.

Region **C** belongs to group A and group B.

Let's practise!

Look at this table and sort the names into the Venn diagram. Decide on a description for each region.

Name	Likes swimming	Likes cycling
Ellie	✗	✔
Ryan	✔	✗
Junior	✔	✔
Abarna	✗	✔
Nirogini	✔	✗
Lisa	✔	✔
Alex	✗	✔

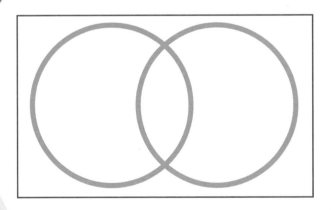

1 Read the question then read it again.

We need to sort the names into groups and decide on definitions or labels for each of these groups.

2 Study the information given.

We can sort the information we have been given into three main groups: Group A (children who like swimming), Group B (children who like cycling) and Group C (children who like swimming and cycling).

3 Sort the information.

Write out the groups on rough paper first.

4 Check your answer against your table.

Check back to make sure you have included all the children in the right groups before completing your answer.

13

Negative numbers

To achieve Level 5, you must understand negative numbers. Be positive!
NEGATIVE NUMBERS ARE EASY. Imagine a thermometer with positive and
negative numbers, and chill out!

Let's practise!

Put these temperatures in order from the coldest to the warmest:

11°C, 5°C, –5°C, –4°C, 2°C, –12°C, 15°C

1 Read the question then read it again.

Negative numbers are colder than positive numbers.

2 Picture the numbers.

Group the numbers.
Negative: (–5, –4, –12)
Positive: (11, 5, 2, 15)

3 Study the numbers.

Draw a number line. Don't forget to include 'zero'. Decide where each number goes.

–12 –5 –4 0 2 5   11 15
                  °C

4 Check your answer.

Are the numbers in order? Check you have used every number.

5 If your answer looks sensible, write it in the box.

If not, go back to step 3 and try again.

| Tips | ★ Numbers are often called INTEGERS. Don't let this put you off. This just means WHOLE numbers without decimals! These are integers: 1, 2, 3, 4 These are not integers: 5.6, 7.8, 11.3 | ★ When thinking of negative numbers, think of a ladder going into a hole in the ground. –2 is higher than –6 so –2 is a larger number than –6 –5 is below –4 so –5 is a smaller number than –4 | 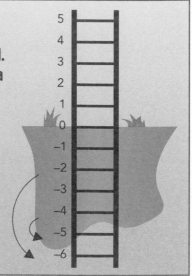 |

Try another question. This time it's a word problem.

Let's practise!

The temperature is –9°C. It rises by 14°C.

What is the new temperature?

1 Read the question then read it again.

'Rises' means getting warmer.

2 Calculate your answer.

–9 –8 –7 –6 –5 –4 –3 –2 –1 0 1 2 3 4 5 6 7 8 9 10

The temperature starts at –9°C. We then need to count up 14 places.

3 Check your answer.

Did you count in the right direction? When adding to a negative number always count towards zero.

4 If your answer checks out, write it in the box.

Our answer is 5°C which is 14°C warmer than –9°C! Brrr...

Practice questions

Use the number line to help you answer these questions.

–25 –24 –23 –22 –21 –20 –19 –18 –17 –16 –15 –14 –13 –12 –11 –10 –9 –8 –7 –6 –5 –4 –3 –2 –1 0 1 2 3 4 5 6 7 8 9 10 11 12 13 14 15 16 17 18 19 20 21 22 23 24 25

1 Circle the lowest temperature in each of these lists:

a) –5°C, 2°C, 7°C, –1°C   b) 5°C, –5°C, –8°C   c) –8°C, –4°C, –10°C

2 Order these integers, starting with the smallest: 6, –7, 16, –18, –16, –20

3 Circle two numbers with a difference of 6: –5, –4, –1, 2, 4

4 The temperature in Moscow is 8°C lower than it is in Oslo. Complete this table.

Temperature in Moscow (°C)		–5		0
Temperature in Oslo (°C)	10		–4	

Adding and subtracting decimals

To achieve Level 5, you need to work with decimal numbers. In addition and subtraction, working with decimals is easy if you remember to line up the decimals!

Let's practise!

> Write in the missing number.
>
> 78.53 + 6.85 + 925.2 = ⬚

1 Read the question then read it again.

78.53 + 6.85 + 925.2 = ?

2 Write the numbers. What do they look like?

78.53 is near 80; 6.85 is near 7. 925.2 is near 900.

3 Study the numbers again and think about them.

The answer will be around 80 + 7 + 900 = 987

4 Set out the sum, lining up the decimal points.

```
   78 . 53
    6 . 85
+ 925 . 2
```

5 Fill in any gaps with zeros.

```
  078 . 53
  006 . 85
+ 925 . 20
```

6 Complete the sum as normal, remembering the decimal point.

```
  078 . 53
  006 . 85
+ 925 . 20
 1010 . 58
    1 2 1
```

7 If your answer looks sensible, write it in the box.

1010.58 is close to our estimate of 987.

Practice questions

1 45.65 − 7.8 = ⬚

2 384.1 − 76.42 = ⬚

3 74.58 + 26.8 = ⬚

4 68.423 + 7.87 = ⬚

Tip	★ Only fill gaps before or after the number with zeros – never put a zero in the middle of a number.

Multiplying and dividing decimals

To achieve Level 5, you need to work with decimal numbers. When multiplying and dividing decimals, you have to know where the decimal point goes!

Let's practise!

Write in the missing number.

$4.45 \times 6.8 = \boxed{}$

1	Read the question then read it again.	$4.45 \times 6.8 = ?$
2	Picture the numbers. What do they look like?	It's nearly 4×7
3	Study the numbers again and think about them.	The answer will be more than 24 (4×6) and less than 35 (5×7).
4	Calculate.	Set out your calculation using the grid method. Don't worry about the decimal point yet.

×	400	40	5	
60	24000	2400	300	= 2 6 7 0 0
8	3200	320	40	= +3 5 6 0
				3 0 2 6 0

5	Remember the rule!	Now count how many digits after the decimal points in the question (3). Three from the right gives 30.260 or 30.26!
6	Check your answer.	So, $4.45 \times 6.8 = 30.26$ 30.26 is just over 30.
7	If your answer looks sensible, write it in the box. If not, go back to step 3.	From step 3 we know our answer should be between 24 and 35. Great!

Practice questions

1. $8.43 \times 7.2 = \boxed{}$

2. $58.6 \div 0.4 = \boxed{}$

3. $24.2 \times 9.8 = \boxed{}$

4. $75.3 \times (34.2 + 5.9) = \boxed{}$

5. $56.4 \div 6 = \boxed{}$

6. $(29.4 - 8.72) \times 4.5 = \boxed{}$

Tip	★ When you multiply, there are the same number of digits after the decimal point in the question as there are in the answer!

Checking your answers

To achieve Level 5, you need to check your answers carefully!

Inverse operations

Remember, adding and subtracting are OPPOSITES. Multiplying and dividing are OPPOSITES. We can use this knowledge to check our calculations quickly.

e.g. $160 - 85 = 75$ CHECK $75 + 85 = 160$
or $252 \div 6 = 42$ CHECK $42 \times 6 = 252$
INVERSE means the same as OPPOSITE.

Let's practise!

$5839 + 823 = \boxed{}$

(1) Read the question then read it again.

5839 add 823

(2) Study the numbers. Picture them in your head.

Picture them on a number line.

(3) Perform the calculation.

$$\begin{array}{r} 5839 \\ +\ 823 \\ \hline 6662 \\ \tiny 1\ 1 \end{array}$$

(4) Does the answer look sensible? If it does, check it using the INVERSE OPERATION.

The opposite of addition is subtraction, so ...

$$\begin{array}{r} {\tiny 5\ 1\ 5\ 1} \\ 6662 \\ -\ 823 \\ \hline 5839 \end{array}$$

(5) Does the check answer match the original sum? If it does, enter the answer in the box. If it doesn't, go back to step 1.

Yes! Our answer is correct!

Practice questions

Do these calculations and then check your answers using the inverse operation.

(1) $36 \times 23 = \boxed{}$

(2) $6454 - 3759 = \boxed{}$

(3) $6453 + 786 = \boxed{}$

(4) $29{,}344 \div 56 = \boxed{}$

| Tip | ★ Always check your answers. Spotting silly mistakes will help you do better in your test! |

Rounding up or down

Another excellent way to check your answers is to round the numbers in the question up or down. Doing this will give you a simple calculation to do and give you a rough answer.

Let's practise!

$$79 \times 22 = \boxed{}$$

(1) Read the question then read it again.

$79 \times 22 = ?$

(2) Study the numbers. Picture them in your head.

Picture them on a number line.

(3) Perform the calculation.

$$
\begin{array}{r}
79 \\
\times \quad 22 \\
\hline
158 \\
1580 \\
\hline
1738 \\
\hline
\end{array}
$$

(4) Now round the numbers and mentally calculate your answer.

79 ROUND TO 80
22 ROUND TO 20
80 × 20 = 1600

(5) Are the answers reasonably close? If so, enter your answer in the box. If not, you must go back to step 1.

Yes, 1738 is close to our estimate of 1600. It looks correct.

Practice questions

Do these calculations and then use the 'rounding up or down' technique to check your answers.

(1) $4763 + 7862 = \boxed{}$

(2) $47 \times 64 = \boxed{}$

(3) $8675 - 749 = \boxed{}$

(4) $558 \div 31 = \boxed{}$

Tips	★ When rounding up or down think of 'friendly' numbers. These are numbers you can work with easily in your head. Some examples are 2, 5, 10, 50, 100 and so on.	★ Get used to doing mental calculations every day. Give your brain 'gym exercises' to do which involve calculating numbers quickly. Darts can be a fun way to do this!

Long multiplication

Long multiplication is an important skill at Level 5.

Let's practise!

Write in the missing number.

578 × 32 = ☐

(1) Read the question then read it again.

578 × 32 = ?

(2) Write the numbers.

578 rounds up to 600 and 32 rounds down to 30.

(3) Study the numbers and think about them.

578 × 32 is roughly 600 × 30, which is 18,000.

(4) To calculate the answer, first multiply by the units.

```
      5 7 8
  ×     3 2
      1 1 5 6   (multiply by 2 first)
        1 1
```

(5) Next, multiply by the tens.

```
      5 7 8
  ×     3 2
      1 1 5 6
    1 7 3 4 0   (then multiply by 30)
        2 2
```

(6) Add your answers together.

```
      5 7 8
  ×     3 2
      1 1 5 6
    1 7 3 4 0
    1 8 4 9 6   (then add your answers)
```

(7) Does the answer look sensible? If it does, write it in the box. If not, go back to step 3.

**18,496 is close to the estimate.
The answer looks correct!**

Practice questions

(1) 375 × 53 = ☐   (2) 385 × 62 = ☐   (3) 396 × 37 = ☐

| Tip | ★ When you multiply by the tens, remember that your answer will end with at least one zero. |

20

Long division

To achieve Level 5, you need to conquer long division.

Let's practise!

Write in the missing number.

987 ÷ 21 = ⬚

1 Read the question then read it again.

987 ÷ 21 = ?

2 Write the numbers. What do they look like?

987 rounds up to 1000 and 21 rounds down to 20.

3 Study the numbers and think about them.

987 ÷ 21 is approximately 1000 ÷ 20 = 50

4 To calculate the answer, start by working out the first part of the division.

$$\begin{array}{r} 4 \\ 21\overline{)987} \\ 84 \\ \hline 14 \end{array}$$

21s into 98 go 4. We subtract 4 × 21 from 98, leaving 14.

5 Bring down the next number and divide again.

$$\begin{array}{r} 47 \\ 21\overline{)987} \\ 84 \\ \hline 147 \\ 147 \\ \hline 0 \end{array}$$

21s into 147 go 7. We subtract 7 × 21 from 147, leaving 0.

6 If your answer looks sensible, write it in the box. If it doesn't, go back to step 2.

47 is very close to our estimate of 50, so it looks correct!

Practice questions

1 810 ÷ 18 = ⬚   **2** 828 ÷ 23 = ⬚   **3** 986 ÷ 34 = ⬚

Tip	★ It helps to write out the times table of the number you are dividing by – it's good for your mental maths too!

Reducing fractions

Reducing fractions is all about finding a fraction's 'common factors'. For example:

$\frac{4}{6}$ can be reduced to $\frac{2}{3}$ (because 4 and 6 can both be divided by 2)

$\frac{3}{9}$ can be reduced to $\frac{1}{3}$ (because 3 and 9 can both be divided by 3)

Let's practise!

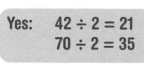 What is $\frac{42}{70}$ in its lowest terms?

① Read the question then read it again.

② Are both numbers divisible by 2?
Yes? Then divide them both by 2.
No? Move to step 4.

Yes: $42 \div 2 = 21$
$70 \div 2 = 35$

③ Look at your new fraction. Can the numbers be divided by 2 again?
Yes? Repeat step 2.
No? Move to step 4.

$\frac{21}{35}$

The numbers cannot be divided by 2 so we move to step 4.

④ Study the fraction. Which number (other than 1) can be divided into both the top and bottom numbers?

Both 21 and 35 can be divided by 7!

⑤ Reduce the fraction. Enter your answer in the box.

$21 \div 7 = 3$ $35 \div 7 = 5$
Our answer is $\frac{3}{5}$

Practice questions

Reduce each of these fractions to their lowest terms (or simplest form):

① $\frac{24}{36}$ ☐   **②** $\frac{36}{60}$ ☐   **③** $\frac{40}{65}$ ☐

④ $\frac{75}{90}$ ☐   **⑤** $\frac{32}{56}$ ☐

Tips	★ Learn to recognise these equivalent fractions.	★ Remember, when you are reducing a fraction ask yourself the following questions:
	$\frac{1}{3} = \frac{2}{6} = \frac{3}{9} = \frac{4}{12} = \frac{5}{15} = \frac{6}{18} = \frac{7}{21}$	• Can both these numbers be divided by 2?
	$\frac{1}{4} = \frac{2}{8} = \frac{3}{12} = \frac{4}{16} = \frac{5}{20} = \frac{6}{24} = \frac{7}{28}$	• Do both these numbers appear in the same times table?
	$\frac{1}{5} = \frac{2}{10} = \frac{3}{15} = \frac{4}{20} = \frac{5}{25} = \frac{6}{30} = \frac{7}{35}$	

Equivalent fractions, decimals and percentages

You need to learn these facts to achieve Level 5. Working round this flow diagram can help make it easy!

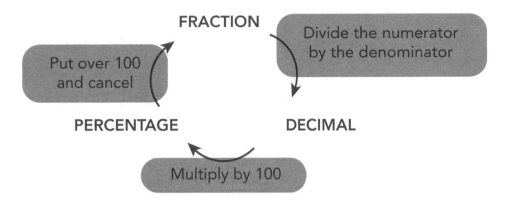

FRACTION

Divide the numerator by the denominator

Put over 100 and cancel

PERCENTAGE   **DECIMAL**

Multiply by 100

Let's practise!

Write $\frac{20}{32}$ as a decimal and a percentage.

1	Read the question then read it again.	We need to change a fraction to a decimal and a percentage.
2	Write the numbers.	$\frac{20}{32}$ reduces to $\frac{5}{8}$.
3	Change the fraction to a decimal.	Divide the numerator by the denominator, $5 \div 8 = 0.625$.
4	Now change the decimal to a percentage.	Multiply the decimal by 100. $0.625 \times 100 = 62.5\%$
5	Does your answer look sensible?	The percentage and decimal are both more than $\frac{1}{2}$. The answer looks correct.

Tip	★ Learn these common percentages, fractions and decimals.

$\frac{1}{2} = 0.5 = 50\%$ $\frac{1}{8} = 0.125 = 12.5\%$ $\frac{1}{3} = 0.33333333... = 33.33333...\%$

$\frac{1}{4} = 0.25 = 25\%$ $\frac{1}{10} = 0.1 = 10\%$ $\frac{2}{3} = 0.66666... = 66.6666...\%$

$\frac{3}{4} = 0.75 = 75\%$

Fractions of amounts

To achieve Level 5, you need to be able to calculate fractions of amounts.

Let's practise!

Write in the missing number.

$\frac{5}{6}$ of 168 = ☐

1 Read the question then read it again.

$\frac{5}{6}$ of 168 = ?

2 Write the numbers.

$\frac{5}{6}$ is close to a whole, so the answer will be a bit less than 168.

3 Divide by the denominator.

The denominator is 6.
168 ÷ 6 = 28

4 Multiply the answer by the numerator.

The numerator is 5.
28 × 5 = 140

5 Does your answer look sensible? If so, write your answer in the box.

140 is a bit less than 168.
The answer looks correct!

Practice questions

Work out these questions **without** a calculator.

1 $\frac{5}{8}$ of 120 ☐

2 $\frac{2}{7}$ of 182 ☐

3 $\frac{5}{9}$ of 207 ☐

4 $\frac{11}{12}$ of 384 ☐

5 $\frac{3}{7}$ of 168 ☐

6 $\frac{7}{9}$ of 144 ☐

7 $\frac{10}{11}$ of 165 ☐

8 $\frac{4}{5}$ of 315 ☐

9 $\frac{8}{15}$ of 450 ☐

10 $\frac{6}{7}$ of 301 ☐

Tip	★ Learn the chant: DIVIDE BY THE BOTTOM AND TIMES BY THE TOP!

Calculating percentages of amounts

Achieved?

At Level 5, you need to be able to work out simple percentages with and without a calculator.

Without a calculator

Let's practise!

> A new mobile phone costs £170. In the sales the price is reduced by 15%. What is the sale price of the mobile?

1 Read the question then read it again. What am I being asked to do?

Find the price of the mobile in the sale.

2 To find the discount, first calculate 10% of the original price.

10% of £170 = £17

3 Now calculate 5% of the original price and add your answers together to find 15%.

**5% is half of 10% so 5% is £8.50
(5%) + (10%) = (15%)
£8.50 + £17.00 = £25.50**

4 Don't forget the next part! What is the SALE price of the mobile?

**The price has been reduced by £25.50.
So the sale price is £170 – £25.50 = £144.50.**

5 Check you have answered the question properly.

What is the sale price of the mobile? After a discount of £25.50 the sale price is £144.50.

With a calculator

You can also work percentages out using a calculator.

> Find 23% of 612.

Let's practise!

1 Read the question and read it again.

23% of 612

2 Write the numbers.

This rounds to 20% of 600, which is 120.

3 Type in the numbers, then press the % key.

 612 × 23 %

4 Does your answer look sensible? If so, write it in the box.

Our answer is 140.76, close to the estimate. Redo the calculation to check it.

Tip	★ To find 1%, find 10% by dividing by 10 and then find 10% of THAT answer. You can work out any % by adding all the 10%, 5% and 1% answers together!

Writing one number as a percentage of another

To achieve Level 5, you need to be able to write one number as a percentage of another.

You can work out many fractions or percentages very easily without a calculator, but sometimes it's not so easy. For example, if you scored 15 out of 30 in your spelling test you should be able to recognise that you got 50% correct. If you improved the following week and got 24 out of 30 then you may need to use your calculator! Calculate as follows:

Key in

You should have the answer 80, which means you scored 80% correct.

Let's practise!

Calculate 48 out of 120 as a percentage.

1	Read the question then read it again.	48 out of 120 means $\frac{48}{120}$
2	Picture the numbers in your head.	48 out of 120 is less than a half, so our answer will be less than 50%.
3	Key in the numbers.	48 ÷ 120
4	Press the % key.	%
5	Does your answer look sensible? If so, put your answer in the box.	Our answer is 40%. It's worth taking a couple of seconds to check by redoing the calculation.

Practice questions

1 Use a calculator to express these fractions as percentages.

a) $\frac{117}{180}$ ☐

b) $\frac{286}{550}$ ☐

c) $\frac{81}{360}$ ☐

2 Express £560 as a percentage of £800. ☐

3 What percentage of 650 kg is 546 kg? ☐

Ratio and proportion

To achieve Level 5, you need to use your ability to cancel (or reduce) fractions to simplify statements about ratio and proportion.

Let's practise!

Have a look at this pattern of tiles:

What is the ratio of blue squares to white squares?

1	Read the question then read it again.	You need to find the ratio.
2	Count the blue and white squares.	There are 8 blue squares and 4 white squares.
3	What is the ratio of blue to white squares?	Blue:white is 8:4.
4	Can you reduce the ratio?	8 and 4 can both be divided by 4 so 8:4 = 2:1.

Now look again at this pattern of tiles:

What is the proportion of blue squares?

1	Read the question then read it again.	Find the proportion of blue squares.
2	Count the blue squares and all the squares.	There are 8 blue squares and 12 squares altogether.
3	What is the proportion of blue squares?	8 squares out of 12 are blue, so the proportion is $\frac{8}{12}$ or 8 in 12.
4	Can you reduce the proportion?	8 and 12 can both be divided by 4 so $\frac{8}{12} = \frac{2}{3}$ or 2 in 3.

Simple formulae

Achieved?

Formulae can be written in words or in letters. To achieve Level 5 you may be required to make up your own formulae in the tests. This is easier than it sounds! Let's start by working through this example.

Let's practise!

Here is a formula for finding the total cost of a pay-as-you-go mobile phone call.

T = £0.25 × M

T = total cost

Each minute costs 25p

M = number of minutes

Now write a formula for finding the cost of one call when the total cost of N calls is £2.25 and the cost of one call is C.

(1) Read the question then read it again.

Lots to read and think about here!

(2) What am I being asked to do?

Write a formula for finding the cost of one call using £2.25, and 'N' and 'C'.

(3) It will help if you say the formula to yourself.

The total cost is £2.25. So … the cost of one call is £2.25, divided by the number of calls, N.

(4) Change your logical statement into a simple formula. Say it to yourself when you write it down.

The cost of one call …	**C**
… is the total cost …	**£2.25**
… divided by (÷) the total number of calls.	**N**

C = £2.25 ÷ N   OR   C = £2.25⁄N

$$C = £2.25 \div N \quad \text{OR} \quad C = \frac{£2.25}{N}$$

Tips	★ Talk through your formula in your head. ★ Think clearly. ★ Take it step by step.	★ It helps to use only letters that relate to the information in the question, e.g. C = cost.

A simple formula is often used to find out the total cost of items bought.

Achieved? ☺ 😐 ☹

In words this formula can be written:

'The total cost is the price of one item multiplied by the number of those items bought.'

In letters this could be written as: **T = N × P**

T = total cost   N = number of items bought   P = price of each item

Practice questions

Use the T = N × P formula to work out these questions.

(**1**) What is the value of **T** if **N** = 8 and **P** = £1.75?

(**2**) What is the value of **N** if **T** = £60 and **P** = £3?

(**3**) What is the value of **P** if **T** = £72 and **N** = 9?

Example question

James and Melissa are playing a number game. James gives Melissa a number which she changes using a rule:

'I take James's number and multiply it by 9 then subtract 8.'

Write a formula to show the process Melissa goes through to get to her answer.

Use J for James's number and M for Melissa's answer.

M = $(J \times 9) - 8$

Practice question

I take James's number and multiply it by 7 then add 7.

(**4**) Now Melissa changes the rule:

Write a formula to show the process Melissa goes through to get to her answer.

Use J for James's number and M for Melissa's answer.

M =

| Tip | ★ If a number and a letter are next to each other, e.g. 4N, it means they are multiplied. Why is the × (multiply) symbol left out? Because it could get confused with the letter x!! |

Using brackets

To achieve Level 5, you must be able to answer questions that contain brackets. This is not a problem – just remember this simple rule:

> Brackets say, "DO ME FIRST!"

Look at this calculation: $2 \times 3 + 4 = 10$

If we add brackets: $2 \times (3 + 4) = 2 \times 7 = 14$

Brackets change the answer!

Let's practise!

Write in the missing number.

$(52 - 29) \times 6 = \boxed{}$

1	Read the question then read it again.	$(52 - 29) \times 6 = ?$
2	Write the numbers. What do they look like?	Rounding the numbers gives $(50 - 30) \times 6$.
3	Study the numbers and think about them.	$(50 - 30) \times 6 = 20 \times 6 = 120$
4	Calculate the numbers in the brackets first.	$52 - 29 = 23$
5	Now complete the calculation.	$(52 - 29) \times 6 = 23 \times 6 = 138$
6	If your answer looks sensible, write it in the box.	138 is close to our estimate of 120. Our answer looks right!

Tip	★ Brackets are very sensitive and need your attention. ALWAYS CALCULATE THE BRACKETS FIRST!

Here is another question with brackets that we can do together. Try the practice questions at the bottom when you think you're ready.

Achieved?

Let's practise!

$$\frac{(34 \times 6) + (272 \times 3)}{30} = \boxed{}$$

1 Read the question then read it again.

What a long calculation! What is it asking?

2 Picture the numbers. What do they look like?

Picture them on a number line. Is this a big number?

3 Calculate the numbers in the brackets first.

×	30	4
6	180	24	= 204

×	200	70	2
3	600	210	6	= 816

204 + 816 = 1020

4 Complete the calculation and then enter the answer.

Divide 1020 by 30.
1020 − 900 (30 × 30)
leaves 120
120 − 120 (4 × 30)
leaves 0
30 + 4 = 34

Practice questions

1 $3.2 \times (3.4 - 1.6) = \boxed{}$

2 $(57 + 135) \times 53 = \boxed{}$

3 $288 \div (92 - 56) = \boxed{}$

4 $(35 \times 42) + \boxed{} = 1800$

5 $\dfrac{(276 \div 12) + (500 - 388)}{5} = \boxed{}$

6 $\dfrac{(35 \times 15) \div (4^2 + 9)}{7} = \boxed{}$

Coordinates

To achieve Level 5 you should be familiar with coordinates and quadrants. Let's try a question to practise what we know!

Let's practise!

Write down the coordinates of each point on this graph.

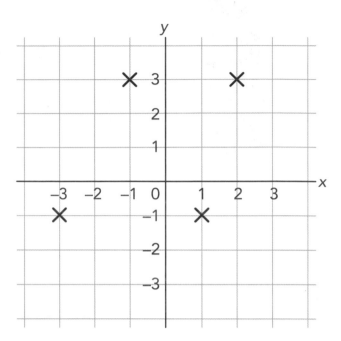

1st quadrant = (__ , __)

2nd quadrant = (__ , __)

3rd quadrant = (__ , __)

4th quadrant = (__ , __)

Remember which quadrant is which!

2nd	1st
3rd	4th

1. Read the question then read it again.

2. Practise your answer.

You can sketch in lines to help you read the coordinates.

3. Check the number of each quadrant.

2nd quadrant	1st quadrant
3rd quadrant	4th quadrant

4. Read off the coordinates in each quadrant.

Remember, read:
ALONG the *x* axis first, then UP or DOWN the *y* axis.
1 (2, 3)   2 (–1, 3)
3 (–3, –1)   4 (1, –1)

5. Double-check and write in your answer.

Check twice! Write once!

Tip	★ Think of going IN the door before going UP or DOWN the stairs.

Achieved?

Using the y axis as a mirror line, draw a reflection of the pentagon in the 1st quadrant.

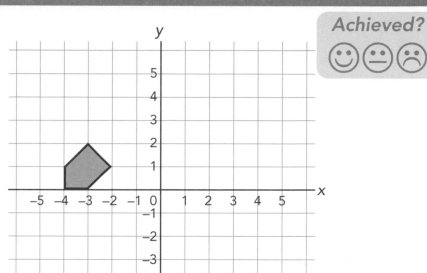

Write the new coordinates of each vertex here.

(__, __)

(__, __)

(__, __)

(__, __)

(__, __)

1 Read the question then read it again.

Note you are being asked to work in the 1st quadrant. 'Vertex' = corner.

2 Practise your answer.

Sketch your pentagon on rough paper first.

3 Note the position of your shape.

Your pentagon must go in the 1st quadrant, mirrored in the *y* axis!

4 Draw your shape on the grid above.

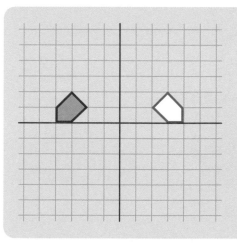

5 Read off your coordinates.

Remember, read ALONG then UP/DOWN: (3, 0), (4, 0), (4, 1), (3, 2), (2, 1)

6 Double-check and write in the answer.

Check twice! Write once!

| Tip | ★ Use a mirror on the y-axis to check the position of your answer. |

Decimal numbers and tables

You should know your tables really well by now. To achieve Level 5, you should practise using your tables to multiply decimals. These are good mental maths questions – so no calculators!

Let's practise!

Write in the missing number.

$0.7 \times 0.08 = \boxed{}$

1 | Read the question then read it again. | $0.7 \times 0.08 = ?$

2 | Write the numbers. | 0.7 is $\frac{7}{10}$ and 0.08 is $\frac{8}{100}$, so we are looking at very small numbers.

3 | Multiply the digits in the question. | $7 \times 8 = 56$

4 | Count the number of digits after the decimal points in the question. | 0.7 has one digit after the decimal point and 0.08 has two – that's three altogether.

5 | Write the answer with that number of digits after the decimal point. | 0.056 has three digits after the decimal point.

6 | Does your answer look sensible? If so, write it in the box. | 0.056 is a very small number. Our answer looks OK.

Practice questions

1 $0.7 \times 6 = \boxed{}$ **2** $0.8 \times 0.008 = \boxed{}$

3 $0.3 \times 0.8 = \boxed{}$ **4** $0.6 \times 0.09 = \boxed{}$

5 $0.004 \times 9 = \boxed{}$ **6** $0.05 \times 7 = \boxed{}$

Number properties

To achieve Level 5, you need to understand some important number properties.

Prime numbers

A prime number always has just **two** factors – itself and one.

The first prime numbers are 2, 3 and 5.

Can you find all the prime numbers up to 100?

Common multiples

Common multiples are multiples that are the same for different numbers.

The multiples of 3 are 3, 6, 9, **12**, 15, 18 …

The multiples of 4 are 4, 8, **12**, 16, 20 …

12 is a common multiple of 3 and 4 because it is on both lists.

Tests of divisibility

Divisibility tests are useful for checking calculations and explaining whether numbers belong in sequences.

A number can be divided by ...	if ...
2	it is even.
3	the sum of its digits is divisible by 3.
4	its last two digits are divisible by 4.
5	it ends in 5 or 0.
6	it is divisible by 2 and 3.
7	No 'ifs'. You have to work this one out the hard way!
8	half of the number can be divided by 4.
9	the sum of its digits is divisible by 9.
10	it ends in 0.

Angles

To achieve Level 5 you need to be able to measure and draw angles and use the correct language for them.

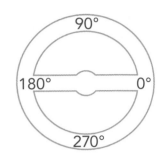

Measuring angles

Use an angle measurer or a protractor to measure these angles.

a)

b)

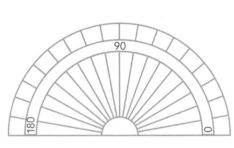

1 Read the question then read it again.

2 Use the curved line to help you find the angle you need to measure.

Where will you measure? Use the curved line to help you.

3 Study the angles.

Estimate and label the angles to help you check your answers:
a) is an acute angle – less than 90°.
b) is an obtuse angle – more than 90° and less than 180°.

4 Measure the angles.

Match up the angle measurer on the vertex (corner) and the lines carefully.

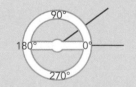

5 Check your answers against your estimates in step 3.

Does each answer match your estimate?

6 If your answer looks sensible, write it in the box.

If not, go back to step 3 and try again.

Drawing angles

Draw your first line (along the page). Then measure the angle you need.

Draw your second line to join the first line at the correct angle you have marked.

Calculating angles

To achieve Level 5 you also need to be able to measure or work out the size of the angles in a triangle and at a point.

Just remember, angles in a triangle add up to 180°.

Let's practise!

Find the unknown angles in these triangles.

a)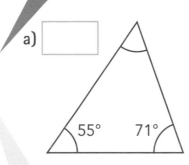

55° 71°

b)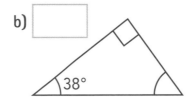

38°

c)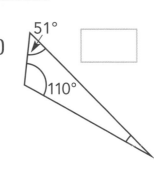

51°

110°

1	Read the question then read it again.	We are given two angles. We need to work out the third angle.
2	Picture the shape and remember the formula.	Angles in a triangle add up to 180°.
3	Study the numbers.	You know two angles so you can work out the third.
4	Calculate your answer.	55° + 71° = 126° 180° − 126° = 54°
5	Check your answer.	Add the three angles together: 55° + 71° + 54° = 180°
6	If your answer checks out, write it in the box.	If not, return to step 3.

Can you work out the remaining two missing angles?

Tips	★ Always turn the paper to make the angles easier to measure. Keep your measurer straight! Make sure you read the correct scale. 	★ Think of a dart board to help you remember the angles in a triangle. One hundred and EIGHTYYYYY! 

Angles at a point

Let's practise!

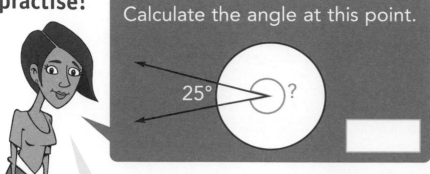

Calculate the angle at this point.

25° ?

1	Read the question then read it again.	'Calculate' usually means you need to work out the answer!
2	Picture the shape. Estimate the angle.	The angle is between 180° and 360°.
3	Remember the formula.	A complete turn = 360°.
4	Study the numbers.	You know one angle so you can work out the other.
5	Calculate your answer.	360° – 25° = 335°
6	Check your answer.	Does it match your estimate?
7	If your answer checks out, write it in the box.	If not, return to step 4.

Practice questions

Calculate angle A in each of the questions.

1

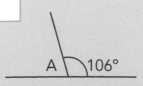

83°
A   36°

2

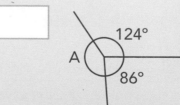

124°
A
86°

3

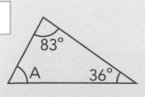

A   106°

4

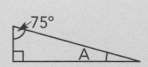

75°
A

Symmetries of 2-D shapes

Achieved?

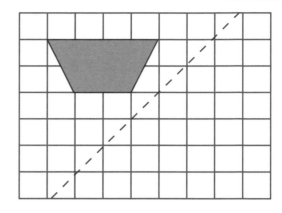

To achieve Level 5, you need to know how to reflect shapes in angled mirrors.

Let's practise!

Draw a reflection of this shape in the mirror line.

1 Read the question then read it again.

You need to reflect the shape.

2 Study the shape.

Trace the shape and mirror line onto tracing paper.

3 Position the reflection.

Turn the tracing paper over. Match the mirror line on the tracing paper to the mirror line in the question. Make sure the shape is now on the other side of the mirror line!

4 Draw the shape in its new position.

Draw over the shape on the tracing paper, then remove the tracing paper and draw the shape accurately with a ruler!

5 Is your answer sensible?

Check the answer using a mirror.

Does this shape have rotational symmetry?

1 Read the question then read it again.

2 Practise your answer.

Trace the shape.

3 Test your answer.

Rotate the shape through 360°. Does the shape look the same in any other position?

   0°   90°   180°   270°

4 Check your answer and write it in.

Yes. The shape looks the same as it does at the start when it is turned through 180°! The shape has rotational symmetry of order 2.

Translating shapes

To achieve Level 5 in maths, you need to know how to translate shapes. Translating shapes is fun – just slide them across the paper. Make sure the shape stays EXACTLY the same though (no turning)!

Let's practise!

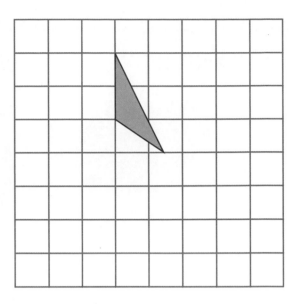

> Sketch the position of the shape after a translation of 3 squares right and 4 squares down.

(1) Read the question then read it again.

'Translation' = slide along

(2) Practise your answer.

Trace the shape and practise the translation before you write in your answer.

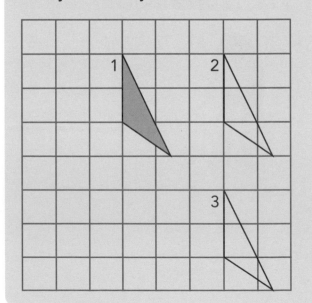

(3) Draw in your final answer.

Double-check first.

Tips	★ 'Translate' means 'slide along'. It is not the same as rotate, which means 'turn around'.	★ Check your answer by tracing the original shape and sliding the tracing paper over your answer. Does the shape match exactly?

Rotation about a point

To achieve Level 5, you need to be able to rotate shapes 90° or 180° about a point. It's easy – just turn the shape round.

Let's practise!

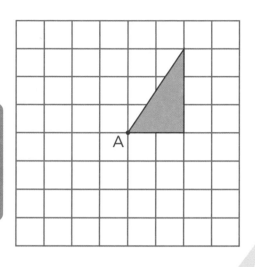

Rotate the triangle 90° anti-clockwise about point A.

1 Read the question then read it again.

'Rotate' means turn.
We have to turn the triangle anti-clockwise through one quarter turn.

2 Picture the shape.

Look at the horizontal and vertical sides and think where they will end up after turning.

3 Rotate the shape.

Trace the shape using tracing paper.
Keep the tracing paper in place and put your pencil on point A. Turn the tracing paper 90° anti-clockwise.

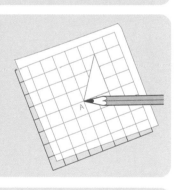

4 Draw the shape in its new position.

Check carefully where the vertices (corners) of the shape end up. If they were on a corner of a grid before, they should be on a corner now too!

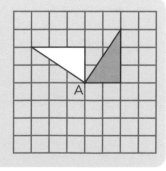

5 Is your answer sensible?

Check the question. We turned the shape through 90° anti-clockwise. The sides on the new shape are exactly the same as on the original shape – the shape looks correct!

| Tips | ★ Remember – 'rotate' just means turn. | ★ DON'T turn your tracing paper over. You will draw a reflection of the shape if you do that! |

Comparing metric to imperial units of measure

To achieve Level 5 you have to answer questions that ask you to compare metric units of measurement (kilometres, grams, litres and centimetres) with imperial units of measurement (miles, pounds, pints). Look at the approximate conversions in the Key facts on page 7.

Let's practise!

Which is longer: 4 feet and 5 inches or 125 cm, and by how much?

1	Read the question then read it again.	**Find how many cm in 4 feet and 3 inches.**
2	Study the units.	**1 foot = 30 cm** **1 inch = 2.5 cm**
3	Convert the units.	**4 feet = 4 × 30 cm = 120 cm** **5 inches = 2.5 × 5 cm = 12.5 cm**
4	Add the units.	**4 feet 5 inches = 120 + 12.5 = 132.5 cm**
5	Answer the question.	**4 feet 5 inches is longer by** **132.5 − 125 = 7.5 cm**

Practice questions

1 Cameron drinks 9 pints of milk a week. How many litres is that?

2 Safi's dog weighs 20 lbs. How many kilograms does it weigh?

Tip	★ **Revision rhymes!** *A metre is just 3 feet 3. It's longer than a yard you see!* *2 and a bit pounds of jam is round about 1 kilo of ham!*

Converting metric units of measure

Achieved?

To achieve Level 5, you have to answer questions that ask you to convert one metric unit to another metric unit.

Let's practise!

Write 6.51 kg as grams.

1 Read the question then read it again.

6.51 kg = _____ g

2 Study the units.

1 kg = 1000 g

3 Calculate the answer.

6.51 × 1000 = 6510

4 Write the correct units.

6510 g

5 If your answer looks sensible, write it in the box.

If not, go back to step 2.

Practice questions

1 A tank holds 50 litres of water. How many millilitres is that?

2 Convert 78.43 m to centimetres.

3 How many kilograms are there in 46,752 g?

Tips	★ Learn the words: milli means 1/1000 kilo means 1000 centi means 1/100	★ Measure things around you to get a feel for the different units.

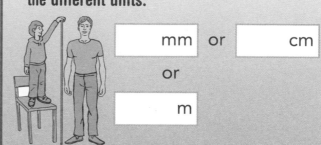

mm or cm

or

m

The area of a rectangle

To achieve Level 5, you need to work out the area of a rectangle. It's easy – just remember this formula:

the area of a rectangle = the length × the width

Let's practise!

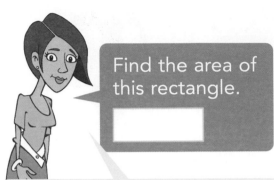

Find the area of this rectangle.

48 cm

22 cm

1 Read the question then read it again.	**TAKE NOTE: you are working with AREA, so there may be a formula!**
2 Remember your formula.	**The area of a rectangle = the length × the width.**
3 Picture the numbers. What do they look like?	**22 cm can be rounded down to 20 cm and 48 cm is nearly 50 cm.**
4 Study the numbers again and think about them.	**We can estimate the answer to be around 1000. (20 × 50 = 1000)**
5 Calculate your answer.	

×	20	2
40	*800*	*80*
8	*160*	*16*

= 880
= +176
‾‾‾‾‾‾
1056

6 Write in your unit of measurement.	**cm squared (cm²) = 1056 cm²**
7 Check your answer against your estimate in step 4.	**1056 is close to 1000.**
8 If your answer looks sensible, write it in the box.	**If not, go back to step 3 and try again.**

Tips	★ When dealing with area, make sure the units are ALWAYS squared, e.g. cm² m² km²	★ Break up complicated shapes into smaller rectangles to make the question easier to answer. Remember to add up the areas of all the rectangles to get your answer!

Let's try another question. Here is a shape you will have to divide up into smaller shapes.

Achieved?

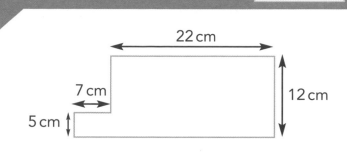

Find the area of this shape.

22 cm

7 cm

5 cm

12 cm

1   Read the question then read it again.

Look for the key words: area and shape.

2   Picture the shape.

It looks like two rectangles joined together!

22 cm

7 cm

5 cm

12 cm

3   Remember the formula.

The area of a rectangle = the length × the width. We need to measure two rectangles.

4   Find the areas of the two rectangles. Then add them together.

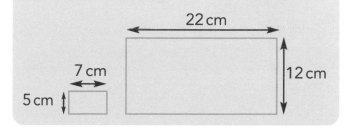

$22 \times 12 = 264$
$7 \times 5 = 35$
Total $= 299$

5   Write in your unit of measurement.

299 cm²

6   If your answer looks sensible, write it in the box.

If not, go back to step 2 and try again.

Practice questions

Try some more questions. If you need to find a missing length, look back at the tips on page 11.

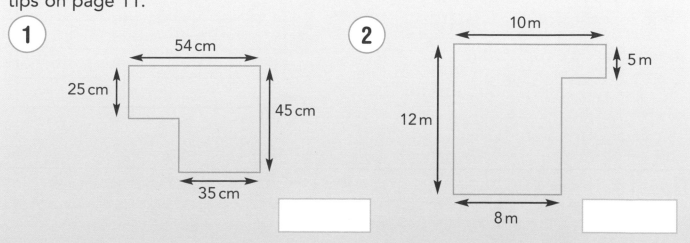

1

54 cm

25 cm

45 cm

35 cm

2

10 m

5 m

12 m

8 m

Approximate readings

To achieve Level 5 you may be asked to give an approximate reading from a measuring instrument, graph, number line or diagram. The readings must be fairly accurate!

Let's practise!

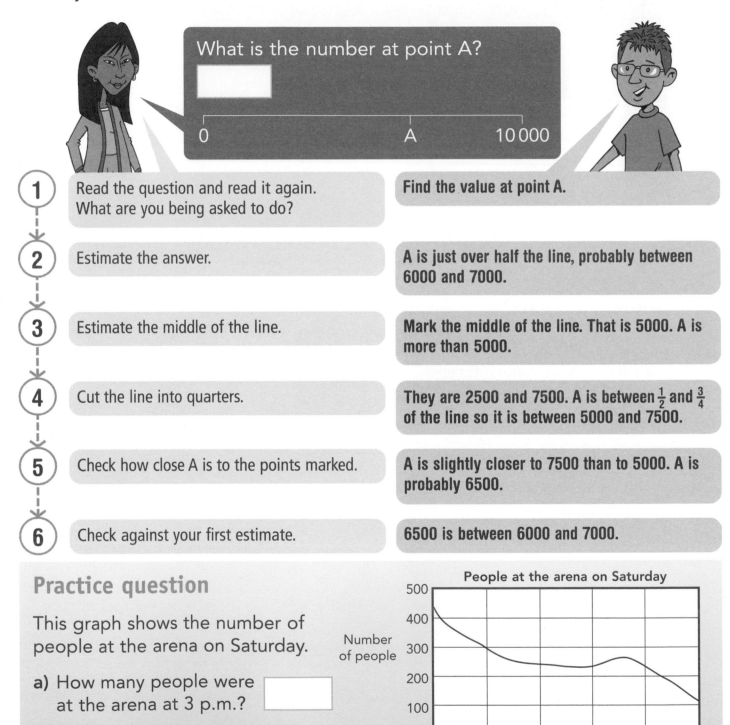

What is the number at point A?

0   A   10 000

1 Read the question and read it again. What are you being asked to do?

Find the value at point A.

2 Estimate the answer.

A is just over half the line, probably between 6000 and 7000.

3 Estimate the middle of the line.

Mark the middle of the line. That is 5000. A is more than 5000.

4 Cut the line into quarters.

They are 2500 and 7500. A is between $\frac{1}{2}$ and $\frac{3}{4}$ of the line so it is between 5000 and 7500.

5 Check how close A is to the points marked.

A is slightly closer to 7500 than to 5000. A is probably 6500.

6 Check against your first estimate.

6500 is between 6000 and 7000.

Practice question

This graph shows the number of people at the arena on Saturday.

a) How many people were at the arena at 3 p.m.?

b) At what time were 200 people at the arena?

People at the arena on Saturday

Number of people

500
400
300
200
100

12 noon   1 p.m.   2 p.m.   3 p.m.   4 p.m.   5 p.m.

Time

| Tip | ★ Draw marks on the diagram for values where you can make a good estimate. Be as accurate as you can – the examiner will be given a range of answers to allow and you must get an answer within that range. |

Finding the mean and median

To achieve Level 5, you need to know how to work out the mean and median of sets of numbers. These are both measures of average (and so is the mode).

To find the mean, you just have to add all the amounts and divide the answer by the number of amounts. For example:

Let's practise!

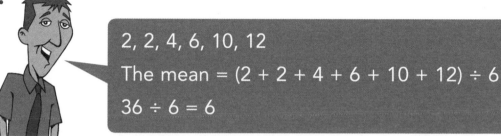

> 2, 2, 4, 6, 10, 12
>
> The mean = (2 + 2 + 4 + 6 + 10 + 12) ÷ 6
>
> 36 ÷ 6 = 6

The median is the **middle number** in a group of numbers. To find the median, put the numbers in order from smallest to largest and find the middle number. For example:

> 48, 23, 67, 94, 12, 73, 88
>
> order is 12, 23, 48, 67, 73, 88, 94
>
> median = 67 (the middle number)

Practice questions

1 Find the mean of these sets of numbers:

a) 3, 7, 13, 8, 5, 6 ◻

b) 35, 86, 64, 69, 21 ◻

c) 345, 874, 65, 364 ◻

d) 573, 100, 876, 52, 138, 97 ◻

2 Find the median of these sets of numbers:

a) 4, 7, 8, 4, 6, 3, 6 ◻

b) 5, 8, 4, 8, 8, 5, 2, 1, 5, 9, 0 ◻

c) 54, 57, 56, 75, 65, 46, 57, 45, 65, 67, 45 ◻

Tips	★ Remember: the mean is what we usually call the 'average'.	★ To help you remember what the median is, think 'small, *medium*, large'. (Median is in the middle!)

Comparing two data sets

To achieve Level 5, you should be able to compare two sets of data using the mean, median, mode and range.

Let's practise!

These are the marks Sam and Kani got in their maths tests. Each test was out of 25.

Sam	23	20	16	22	12	21
Kani	19	24	18	21	20	24

Use the range and mean to work out who has the better results.

1 Read the question then read it again.

Compare the range and mean.

2 Think about the numbers.

They both had weeks when each did better than the other.

3 Calculate the ranges.

Sam: 23 − 12 = 11
Kani: 24 − 18 = 6

4 Calculate the means.

Sam: (23 + 20 + 16 + 22 + 12 + 21) ÷ 6 = 19
Kani: (19 + 24 + 18 + 21 + 20 + 24) ÷ 6 = 21

5 Compare the results.

Sam: range of 11 and a mean of 19
Kani: range of 6 and a mean of 21

6 What do the results mean?

Kani had a higher mean, so her average mark was higher than Sam's. Sam had a higher range than Kani, so his marks were not consistent. Some were very good and some were bad! This means that Kani's results were better.

7 Does your answer look sensible?

Look back at the data. Kani always got good marks. The answer looks correct.

Conversion graphs

To get a Level 5 you need to look at graphs like the one below and answer questions about them.

Let's practise!

These road signs are in miles. Use the conversion graph to rewrite the road signs in kilometres.

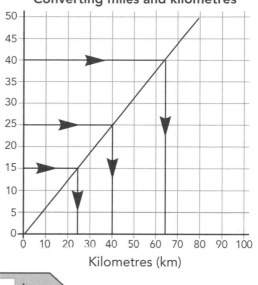

Converting miles and kilometres

Miles / Kilometres (km)

Exeter 40 miles → Exeter _____ km

Torquay 25 miles → Torquay _____ km

Newton Abbot 15 miles → Newton Abbot _____ km

1 Read the question then read it again.

Conversion graph tells us that we need to convert values.

2 Be methodical.

Exeter
- We need to change 40 miles into kilometres.
- Go up the *y* axis (miles) and find 40.
- Mark this point on the *y* axis with your pencil.
- Go across to the conversion line and make another mark.
- Now go down to find out the value in kilometres.

Our answer is nearly halfway between 60 and 70, so we can estimate 64 km! Now repeat for Torquay and Newton Abbot.

3 Does the answer look sensible? If so, fill in the answer boxes.

Check your answers carefully on the graph before writing them in the boxes. The test marker is looking for an EXACT answer.

Practice questions

The exchange rate for pounds to stars is £1 = ★1.6. Using the graph above to help you, draw a new graph to convert pounds to stars. Use the graph to find out how much you would receive when you exchange:

a) £55 = ★ _____

b) £40 = ★ _____

Pie charts

Pie charts are an important part of Level 5.

Pie charts are a good way of showing fractions, percentages or proportions. They are an excellent way of showing information quickly and clearly ... as long as you know what to look for! Get used to seeing what the slices 'look like' so you can instantly recognise the proportions of a whole. It is worth drawing circles and practising dividing them into equal parts like $\frac{1}{3}$s, $\frac{1}{2}$s, $\frac{1}{5}$s.

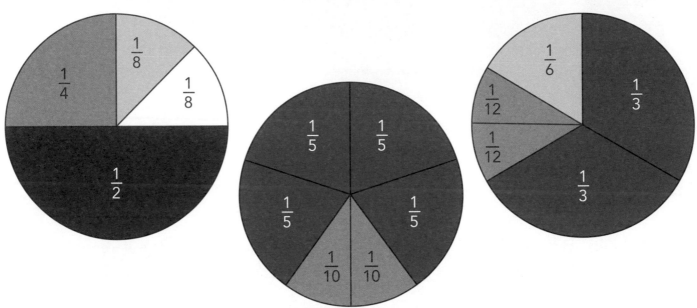

Practice questions

Use the pie charts above to estimate what fraction of the population of Birmingham is:

a) over 75

b) under 40

c) 21 and under

Ages of the population of Birmingham

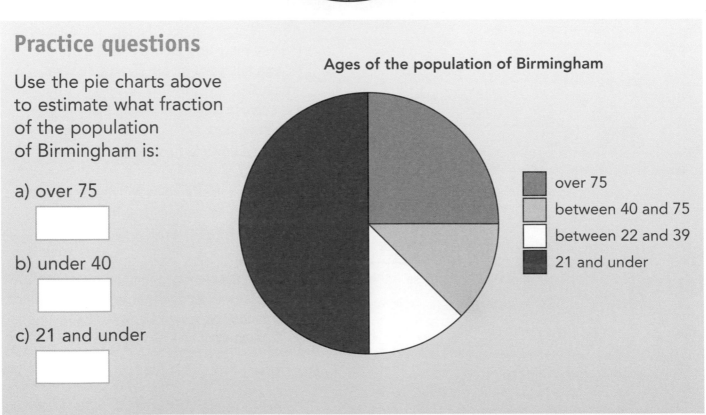

- over 75
- between 40 and 75
- between 22 and 39
- 21 and under

Tips	★ Be VERY careful when reading scales or axes. You may be asked to find values BETWEEN lines on the scale. A test marker would want to know if you can find the EXACT answer.	★ Always draw graphs and read graphs carefully and accurately. A sharp pencil, straight ruler and steady hand are essential!

Probability

To achieve Level 5, you need to understand probability.

The probability scale is a way of showing how likely something is to happen on a scale of 0 to 1.

| 0 | $\frac{1}{4}$ | $\frac{1}{2}$ | $\frac{3}{4}$ | 1 |
| Impossible | Less likely | Even chance | More likely | Certain |

Here are some examples:

| 0 | $\frac{1}{4}$ | $\frac{1}{2}$ | $\frac{3}{4}$ | 1 |
| Pacific Ocean turning to custard | | Coin landing on heads | | Sun rising tomorrow |

You will have to answer two types of question about probability scales.

Let's practise!

| 0 | $\frac{1}{4}$ | $\frac{1}{2}$ | $\frac{3}{4}$ | 1 |
| Impossible | Less likely | Even chance | More likely | Certain |

Place this statement on the scale above using an arrow and a label.

'It will rain at least once during April.'

(1) Read the question then read it again.

Reading is important here as there are more words than numbers!

(2) Picture the question in your mind.

Imagine the time of year. What's he saying? Oh yes, April showers ...

(3) Picture the question again.

Is it certain to rain in April? No, but it's possible. It's not impossible, and I would say there is more than an even chance it will rain in April.

(4) Does the answer look sensible? If so, place your arrow on the scale.

I'll put my arrow pointing towards 'more likely' as that seems most sensible.

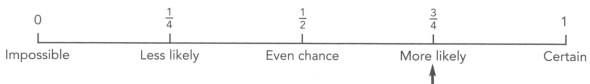

| 0 | $\frac{1}{4}$ | $\frac{1}{2}$ | $\frac{3}{4}$ | 1 |
| Impossible | Less likely | Even chance | More likely | Certain |

↑

'It will rain at least once during April.'

Now let's try a probability question that asks for an answer with numbers.

These coloured balls were placed in a bag:

5 pink   30 blue   2 green   3 brown

Estimate the chance that the first ball to be taken out of the bag will be a blue ball and mark it on the probability scale.

1 Read the question then read it again.

Words and numbers to think about.
What is the question asking you to do?

2 Picture the question in your mind.

Try to picture the different coloured balls going into the bag.

3 Add up the total number of balls.

$5 + 30 + 2 + 3 = 40$

4 How many of them are blue?

There are 30 blue balls. So there are 30 blue balls out of 40.

5 Express your probability as a fraction, decimal or percentage. This is important!

This can be expressed as a fraction, percentage or decimal:
$\frac{3}{4}$ 75%   0.75

6 Decide where to place your arrow.

Draw the arrow three quarters of the way along the line. Be accurate here because the probability scale is clearly marked.

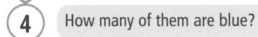

0	$\frac{1}{4}$	$\frac{1}{2}$	$\frac{3}{4}$	1
Impossible	Less likely	Even chance	More likely	Certain

First ball will be blue.

Practice questions

1 On a dice, what is the probability of throwing a 6?

2 James spins this spinner.

What is the probability he gets a 3?

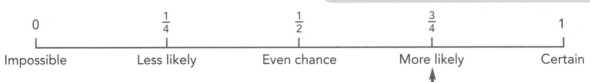

Tips	★ When throwing a dice there is an EQUAL chance of rolling any of the numbers. When tossing a coin there is an EQUAL chance of getting heads or tails.	★ If you are not marking a probability on a scale, you must present it as a *fraction, decimal* or *percentage*.

Solving problems

To achieve Level 5, you need to be able to solve all kinds of maths problems.

The reason for learning all the different mathematical skills (multiplying, dividing, measuring, estimating, and so on) is so you can use them to solve mathematical problems.

Imagine learning all the shots in tennis – like the serve, the volley, the backhand and forehand – but never actually getting to play a game! Only by using your shots in a match will you learn to be a tennis player. Likewise, only by using your mathematical skills will you learn to be a mathematician!

The flow chart on page 54 is designed to guide you when tackling a maths problem. It will help organise your thinking, but it won't tell you the answer – that's for you to work out for yourself.

The next few pages contain problems for you to solve. Work through the examples first and then have a go at the practice questions using the flow chart approach.

Good luck!

Problem solving

Number

These questions are all about your number skills. You must use them in the right way though!

Shape and space

These questions all require you to use your knowledge about shapes, both 2-D and 3-D.

Measures

These questions are all about real situations: going on a journey, the amount of milk a family drinks in a week, and so on.

Handling data

These questions often ask you to find out information from a table or chart. They will also ask you to explain how you found out the answer!

The problem-solving flow chart

(1) Read the question then read it again.

Read the question carefully. Twice. Let the words and numbers 'sink in'.

(2) Write the numbers and highlight any key words.

Write down any numbers and key words. It might help to draw a picture or diagram.

(3) Can you estimate an answer?

This depends on the question. Try to estimate using the numbers and words you jotted down in step 2.

(4) Which calculations do you need to do?

Work out if you need to use +, −, × or ÷ and check if you need to do more than one calculation.

(5) Work out the problem.

Do any calculations needed. Make sure you are answering the problem.

(6) Is your answer sensible?

Read the question again and check that your answer is realistic. If not, go back to step 2.

Tips	★ Remember your 'checking the answer' skills. ★ Think clearly and write clearly. ★ Present your work so it shows what you have done. ★ Work step by step. ★ Make a problem easier (e.g. 'Find 24 lots of 6.' Try finding 4 lots first then 20 lots).	★ Take a reasonable guess at what you think might happen. ★ Think HOW you are working. Change your method if something isn't working. ★ Look for patterns in your maths.

Solving number problems

Let's practise!

The numbers in row 2 of this triangle of pool balls have been found from the two numbers directly above them using a rule. Fill in the missing numbers and write the rule.

Row 1 ⟨84⟩ ⟨72⟩ ⟨88⟩ ⟨44⟩
Row 2 ⟨78⟩ ⟨80⟩ ⟨66⟩
Row 3
Row 4

Rule: _____

1 Read the question then read it again.

There are two things to do to complete this question – 'find the missing numbers' and 'write the rule'.

2 Picture the words and numbers. What do they mean?

How are these numbers 'linked'? When we have worked it out, we need to explain how.

3 Highlight key words and phrases.

'Numbers in row 2'; 'found from the two numbers directly above'

4 Can you estimate an answer?

No, because the answer is not immediately obvious.

5 What calculations do you need to do?

Work step by step. Start with 84 and 72. What do we have to do to get 78?
$84 + 72 = ?$ or $84 - 72 = ?$

6 What is the answer to your calculations? Show how you got your answer.

$84 + 72 = 156$ and $84 - 72 = 12$
Look at our answers. Can we see any 'link' with 78? Yes! 156 is double 78 or 78 is half 156. We have found the rule!

7 What is the answer to the original problem? Write it in full.

The rule is add the two numbers together and divide the total by two. We can also fill in the missing numbers.
$(78 + 80) ÷ 2 = 79$ and $(80 + 66) ÷ 2 = 73$
so $(79 + 73) ÷ 2 = 76$

8 Is your answer a sensible one?

Yes, we can test our rule throughout the triangle. It works!

55

Practice questions

Use the flow chart to help you solve these number problems.

1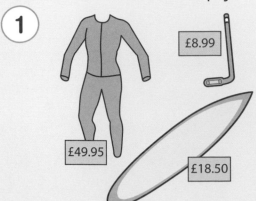

£8.99

£49.95

£18.50

Talib had £100. He chose a surfboard and a wetsuit. He received a 20% discount off the total price. How much money did he have left?

2 There are 3 girls for every 4 boys in Class 6A. If there are 28 children in the class, how many of them are girls?

3 Daniel starts at zero and counts in steps of 9.

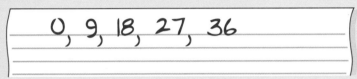

0, 9, 18, 27, 36

a) He says the number 563 will be in his sequence.

  Is he correct?   YES   NO

  Explain how you know.

b) What is the first number greater than 700
   that would be in his sequence?

4 Put the numbers 1 to 9 into this grid so that the sum of the numbers of the columns, rows and the diagonals each equal 15. Investigate other magic squares.

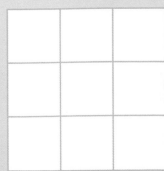

Solving measures problems

Let's practise!

Here is a list of ingredients for Jimmy's jam tarts. It makes 12 jam tarts.

180 g plain flour   6 teaspoons water

80 g butter   120 g strawberry jam

12 fresh strawberries

Jimmy is having some extra friends round for tea and wants to make 15 of his special tarts. Can you change the amount of each ingredient so he cooks enough tarts?

1 Read the question then read it again.	**Change the amounts of 5 ingredients …**
2 Picture the words and numbers. What do they mean?	**We could draw each item.**
3 Highlight key words and phrases.	**Change the amounts so there are enough tarts for 15 instead of 12 … That's an increase of 25%!**
4 Can you estimate an answer?	**Not easy as there are lots of ingredients, but we know we are adding a 'quarter as much again' to each ingredient.**
5 What calculations do you need to do?	**25% of each – 180 g, 80 g, 6 teaspoons, 120 g, 12 strawberries.**
6 What is the answer to your calculations? Show how you got your answer.	**25% of 180 g = 45 g** **25% of 80 g = 20 g** **25% of 6 teaspoons = 1.5 teaspoons** **25% of 120 g = 30 g** **25% of 12 strawberries = 3 strawberries** **Add these to the amounts for 12.**
7 What is the answer to the original problem? Write it in full.	**Jimmy would need 225 g of plain flour, 100 g of butter, 7.5 teaspoons of water, 150 g of jam and 15 strawberries.**
8 Is your answer a sensible one?	**Yes, we have increased the ingredients by the correct amounts.**

Practice questions

1

A tub contains 12 identical cups and weighs 900 g.

The empty tub weighs 36 g.

What is the weight of each cup?

2

perimeter = 498 mm

(not to scale)

A square has a perimeter of 498 mm.

What is the length of each side in cm?

3

Hannah has a jigsaw puzzle that is 83 cm long and 30 cm wide. If each puzzle piece is 3 mm thick, what is the volume of the jigsaw puzzle?

4 During a holiday, the Chang family put 28 litres of petrol of petrol into the car 6 times. When they left on holiday, the car held 24 litres of petrol. When they returned home it held 13 litres of petrol. How much petrol did they use altogether on holiday?

Solving shape and space problems

Let's try a tricky shape and space problem.

Let's practise!

How many equilateral triangles can you see in this diagram?

Show your method:

| 1 | Read the question then read it again. | Study the words and the shape. Think past the obvious. |

| 2 | Picture the words and numbers. What do they mean? | It would help to sketch the shape on paper. You will need to work in a logical, methodical way. Think step by step! |

| 3 | Highlight key words and phrases. | How many. We are going to need the exact number of triangles to be correct. Miss one and we're wrong! |

| 4 | Can you estimate an answer? | We can see 17 in front of us (16 little ones and the big one). 5 hidden, 22 in total. |

| 5 | What calculations do you need to do? | Work in a logical way using a table. How many '1–triangles' are there? How many '4–triangles' are there? And so on … |

| 6 | What is the answer to your calculations? Show how you got your answer. | |

Number of smaller triangles in the big triangle	1	4	9	16	Total
Quantity seen	16	7	3	1	27

| 7 | What is the answer to the original problem? Write it in full. | We can see 27 equilateral triangles in the diagram. |

| 8 | Is your answer a sensible one? | It looks sensible because we worked in a step-by-step way. Our estimate was quite close and a logical approach has given us the correct answer. |

Practice questions

1 Rachel uses square slabs to make a path with this pattern.

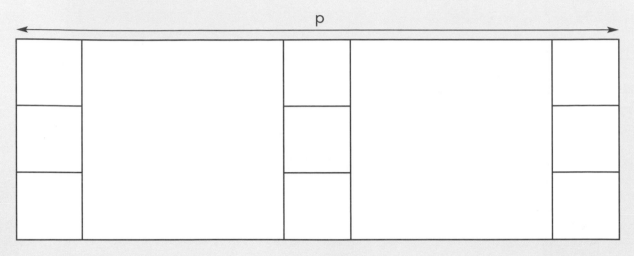

If the large square has a side length of 84 cm, what is length p?

2 This tile is turned 90° clockwise.

Complete the tile in its new position.

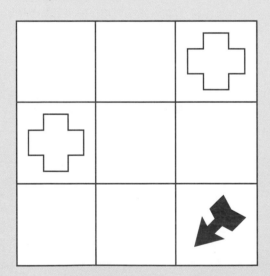
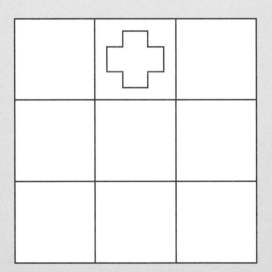

3 A quadrilateral has one pair of parallel sides and one pair of equal sides.

Name the shape.

Learning objectives for Primary Mathematics

This chart allows you to see the progression from Year 6 to Year 7 for each strand following the new Primary Mathematics Framework.

The key objectives are in **bold type**.

Attainment target and Strand	Year 6	Year 7
Using and applying mathematics	Solve multi-step problems, and problems involving fractions, decimals and percentages; choose and use appropriate calculation strategies at each stage, including calculator use	Solve problems by breaking down complex calculations into simpler steps; choose and use operations and calculation strategies appropriate to the numbers and context; try alternative approaches to overcome difficulties; present, interpret and compare solutions
	Tabulate systematically the information in a problem or puzzle; identify and record the steps or calculations needed to solve it, using symbols where appropriate; interpret solutions in the original context and check their accuracy	Represent information or unknown numbers in a problem, for example in a table, formula or equation; explain solutions in the context of the problem
	Suggest, plan and develop lines of enquiry; collect, organise and represent information, interpret results and review methods; identify and answer related questions	Develop and evaluate lines of enquiry; identify, collect, organise and analyse relevant information; decide how best to represent conclusions and what further questions to ask
	Represent and interpret sequences, patterns and relationships involving numbers and shapes; suggest and test hypotheses; construct and use simple expressions and formulae in words then symbols (e.g. the cost of c pens at 15 pence each is 15c pence)	Generate sequences and describe the general term; use letters and symbols to represent unknown numbers or variables; represent simple relationships as graphs
	Explain reasoning and conclusions, using words, symbols or diagrams as appropriate	Explain and justify reasoning and conclusions, using notation, symbols and diagrams; find a counter-example to disprove a conjecture; use step-by-step deductions to solve problems involving shapes
Number and algebra Counting and understanding number	Find the difference between a positive and a negative integer, or two negative integers, in context	Compare and order integers and decimals in different contexts
	Use decimal notation for tenths, hundredths and thousandths; partition, round and order decimals with up to three places, and position them on the number line	Order a set of fractions by converting them to decimals
	Express a larger whole number as a fraction of a smaller one (e.g. recognise that 8 slices of a 5-slice pizza represents $\frac{8}{5}$ or $1\frac{3}{5}$ pizzas); simplify fractions by cancelling common factors; order a set of fractions by converting them to fractions with a common denominator	Recognise approximate proportions of a whole and use fractions and percentages to describe and compare them, for example when interpreting pie charts
	Express one quantity as a percentage of another (e.g. express £400 as a percentage of £1000); find equivalent percentages, decimals and fractions	**Use ratio notation, reduce a ratio to its simplest form and divide a quantity into two parts in a given ratio; solve simple problems involving ratio and direct proportion (e.g. identify the quantities needed to make a fruit drink by mixing water and juice in a given ratio)**
	Solve simple problems involving direct proportion by scaling quantities up or down	
Number and algebra Knowing and using number facts	**Use knowledge of place value and multiplication facts to 10 × 10 to derive related multiplication and division facts involving decimals (e.g. 0.8 × 7, 4.8 ÷ 6)**	Consolidate rapid recall of number facts, including multiplication facts to 10 × 10 and the associated division facts
	Use knowledge of multiplication facts to derive quickly squares of numbers to 12 × 12 and the corresponding squares of multiples of 10	Recognise the square roots of perfect squares to 12 × 12
	Recognise that prime numbers have only two factors and identify prime numbers less than 100; find the prime factors of two-digit numbers	Recognise and use multiples, factors, divisors, common factors, highest common factors and lowest common multiples in simple cases
	Use approximations, inverse operations and tests of divisibility to estimate and check results	**Make and justify estimates and approximations to calculations**

61

Attainment target and Strand	Year 6	Year 7
Number and algebra Calculating	Calculate mentally with integers and decimals: U.t ± U.t, TU × U, TU ÷ U, U.t × U, U.t ÷ U	Understand how the commutative, associative and distributive laws, and the relationships between operations, including inverse operations, can be used to calculate more efficiently; use the order of operations, including brackets
	Use efficient written methods to add and subtract integers and decimals, to multiply and divide integers and decimals by a one digit integer, and to multiply two-digit and three-digit integers by a two-digit integer	Consolidate and extend mental methods of calculation to include decimals, fractions and percentages
	Relate fractions to multiplication and division (e.g. 6 ÷ 2 = ½ of 6 = 6 × ½); express a quotient as a fraction or decimal (e.g. 67 ÷ 5 = 13.4 or 13²⁄₅); find fractions and percentages of whole-number quantities (e.g. ⅝ of 96, 65% of £260)	Use standard column procedures to add and subtract integers and decimals, and to multiply two-digit and three-digit integers by a one-digit or two-digit integer; extend division to dividing three-digit integers by a two-digit integer
	Use a calculator to solve problems involving multi-step calculations	Calculate percentage increases or decreases and fractions of quantities and measurements (integer answers)
		Use bracket keys and the memory of a calculator to carry out calculations with more than one step; use the square root key
Shape, space and measures Understanding shape	Describe, identify and visualise parallel and perpendicular edges or faces; use these properties to classify 2-D shapes and 3-D solids	Use correctly the vocabulary, notation and labelling conventions for lines, angles and shapes
	Make and draw shapes with increasing accuracy and apply knowledge of their properties	Extend knowledge of properties of triangles and quadrilaterals and use these to visualise and solve problems, explaining reasoning with diagrams
	Visualise and draw on grids of different types where a shape will be after reflection, after translation, or after rotation through 90° or 180° about its centre or one of its vertices	**Know the sum of angles on a straight line, in a triangle and at a point, and recognise vertically opposite angles**
	Use coordinates in the first quadrant to draw, locate and complete shapes that meet given properties	Use all four quadrants to find coordinates of points determined by geometric information
	Estimate angles, and use a protractor to measure and draw them, on their own and in shapes; calculate angles in a triangle or around a point	Identify all the symmetries of 2-D shapes; transform images using ICT
		Construct a triangle given two sides and the included angle
Shape, space and measures Measuring	**Select and use standard metric units of measure and convert between units using decimals to two places (e.g. change 2.75 litres to 2750ml, or vice versa)**	Convert between related metric units using decimals to three places (e.g. convert 1375mm to 1.375m, or vice versa)
	Read and interpret scales on a range of measuring instruments, recognising that the measurement made is approximate and recording results to a required degree of accuracy; compare readings on different scales, for example when using different instruments	**Solve problems by measuring, estimating and calculating; measure and calculate using imperial units still in everyday use; know their approximate metric values**
	Calculate the perimeter and area of rectilinear shapes; estimate the area of an irregular shape by counting squares	Calculate the area of right-angled triangles given the lengths of the two perpendicular sides, and the volume and surface area of cubes and cuboids
Handling data	Describe and predict outcomes from data using the language of chance or likelihood	**Understand and use the probability scale from 0 to 1; find and justify probabilities based on equally likely outcomes in simple contexts**
	Solve problems by collecting, selecting, processing, presenting and interpreting data, using ICT where appropriate; draw conclusions and identify further questions to ask	Explore hypotheses by planning surveys or experiments to collect small sets of discrete or continuous data; select, process, present and interpret the data, using ICT where appropriate; identify ways to extend the survey or experiment
	Construct and interpret frequency tables, bar charts with grouped discrete data, and line graphs; interpret pie charts	Construct, interpret and compare graphs and diagrams that represent data, for example compare proportions in two pie charts that represent different totals
	Describe and interpret results and solutions to problems using the mode, range, median and mean	Write a short report of a statistical enquiry and illustrate with appropriate diagrams, graphs and charts, using ICT as appropriate; justify the choice of what is presented

Answers

Level 4 – The Tricky Bits

Level 4 – The Tricky Bits

Page 9 – Predicting sequences
1) 59, 71 2) 7, 17 3) 1, –3 4) 11, 17

Page 11 – The 24-hour clock
1) 4 hours 45 mins 2) 7 hours 27 minutes 3) 03:07

Page 12 – Reading scales
A = 0.8 km or 800 m B = 1.3 km or 1300 m C = 2.6 km or 2600 m

Page 13 – Venn diagrams
Group A: Ryan, Nirogini; Group B: Ellie, Abarna, Alex; Group C: Junior, Lisa

Number and algebra

Page 15 – Negative numbers
1) a) –5°C b) –8°C c) –10°C
2) –20, –18, –16, –7, 6, 16
3) –4 and 2 circled
4)

Temperature in Moscow (°C)	2	–5	–12	0
Temperature in Oslo (°C)	10	3	–4	8

Page 16 – Adding and subtracting decimals
1) 37.85 2) 307.68 3) 101.38 4) 76.293

Page 17 – Multiplying and dividing decimals
1) 60.696 2) 146.5 3) 237.16 4) 3019.53 5) 9.4 6) 93.06

Page 18 – Checking your answers – inverse operations
1) 828 2) 2695 3) 7239 4) 524

Page 19 – Checking your answers – rounding up or down
1) 12,625 2) 3008 3) 7926 4) 18

Page 20 – Long multiplication
1) 19,875 2) 23,870 3) 14,652

Page 21 – Long division
1) 45 2) 36 3) 29

Page 22 – Reducing fractions
1) $\frac{2}{3}$ 2) $\frac{3}{5}$ 3) $\frac{8}{13}$ 4) $\frac{5}{6}$ 5) $\frac{4}{7}$

Page 24 – Fractions of amounts
1) 75 2) 52 3) 115 4) 352 5) 72
6) 112 7) 150 8) 252 9) 240 10) 258

Page 26 – Writing one number as a percentage of another
1) a) 65% b) 52% c) 22.5%
2) 70% 3) 84%

Page 29 – Simple formulae
1) T = £14 2) N = 20 3) P = £8 4) Formula M = (J x 7) + 7

Page 31 – Using brackets
1) 5.76 2) 10,176 3) 8 4) 330 5) 27 6) 3

Page 34 – Decimal numbers and tables

1) 4.2   2) 0.0064   3) 0.24   4) 0.054   5) 0.036   6) 0.35

Page 35 – Number properties

2, 3, 5, 7, 11, 13, 17, 19, 23, 29, 31, 37, 41, 43, 47, 53, 59, 61, 67, 71, 73, 79, 83, 89, 97

Shape, space and measures

Page 36 – Angles

a) 30°   b) 115°

Page 37 – Calculating angles

b) 52°   c) 19°

Page 38 – Angles at a point

1) 61°   2) 150°   3) 74°   4) 15°

Page 42 – Converting metric to imperial units of measure

1) 5 litres (accept 4.5 litres)   2) 9–10 kilograms

Page 43 – Converting metric units of measure

1) 50,000 ml   2) 7843 cm   3) 46.752 kg

Page 45 – The area of a rectangle

1) 2050 cm²   2) 106 m²

Page 46 – Approximate readings

a) 230–240 inclusive   b) 4:16–4:25 inclusive

Handling data

Page 47 – Finding the mean and median

1) a) 7   b) 55   c) 412   d) 306
2) a) 6   b) 5   c) 57

Page 49 – Conversion graphs

a) ★ 88   b) ★ 64

Page 50 – Pie charts

a) $\frac{1}{4}$ b) $\frac{5}{8}$ c) $\frac{1}{2}$

Page 52 – Probability

1) $\frac{1}{6}$ 2) $\frac{3}{8}$

Using and applying mathematics

Page 56 – Solving number problems

1) £45.24   2) 12
3) a) No, 563 is not divisible by 9 because its digits add up to 14 (which is not divisible by 9)
   b) 702

4)

8	1	6
3	5	7
4	9	2

Note: There are other possible solutions which are rearrangements of this grid. Check with your teacher if you need help.

Page 58 – Solving measures problems

1) 72 g   2) 12.45 cm   3) 747 cm³   4) 179 litres

Page 60 – Solving shape and space problems

1) 252 cm   2)   3) trapezium